Love, God

Hearing God's Heart

In His Word

Lisa DeVinney

ISBN: 979-8-89686-515-5

Cover design by Danni and Lisa DeVinney

DEDICATION

To my Shepherd, Lord, Savior, and Friend Jesus
who calls me by name and invites me
to spend precious time at His nail-scarred feet,
listening to His voice singing over me.
What joy to be His and to call Him mine!

"…the sheep recognize His voice and come to him.
He calls his own sheep by name and leads them out.
After he has gathered his own flock, he walks ahead of them,
and they follow him because they know his voice."
John 10:3-4 NLT

With love,

Lisa

TABLE of CONTENTS

INTRODUCTION

Don't you just love getting personal cards and letters in the mail? It's such a joy knowing someone was thinking of you and took the time to write down their thoughts to share with you.

What if, instead of reading The Bible as an instruction manual or rule book, we read it as a personal love letter from God? After all, His love for us is poured into every word on every page because that's just who He is.

Yet, I hear time and time again, "I just can't understand it. It's so hard to read."

If you've felt that way yourself or know someone who has, *Love, God* is written especially for you! It is in no way intended to replace Scripture. My hope is that, instead, it will inspire you to open the Word for yourself. This devotional is meant to come alongside your scripture reading, and share it from a new perspective, making it feel a little more personal...like God is speaking directly to you. After all, He is. All the time.

It's my prayer that if you happen to be a new believer, *Love, God*, will lead you toward discovering the joy of hearing your Shepherd's voice, maybe for the first time.

I pray that if you don't yet know Jesus, you might get a glimpse of what it's like to have a relationship...a truly personal relationship with the One who desires to be the Shepherd of your soul. And in doing so, you would have the opportunity to taste and see that the Lord really is good.

And for you seasoned believers, my prayer is that *Love, God* will remind you how it feels to delight in spending time with your Shepherd, Savior, and Friend.

———

At the end of each day's devotion, you'll find four sections for reflection -

Digging Deeper includes the main passage from which that day's thoughts were taken. In addition, there are extra verses and passages relating to the day's devotion. If other Scriptures come to mind as you read, I encourage you to make a note of them as well. Then be sure to go back and read them. Consider what more God may want to say to you through those verses.

They may be the most important ones of the day for you!

Questions to Consider asks general questions to think about as you read the Bible verses. These questions will be repeated throughout the devotional.

Personal Reflection encourages you to reflect more deeply on what you've read or what might have hit you just a little differently than previous times reading those same passages. Has God used that day's message to put His finger on something in your own life that needs more careful thought and prayer? And what have you learned about yourself in relationship to your Heavenly Father and others?

Room to Respond finishes each day with the encouragement to make things personal. There's space to rewrite a passage or verse, inserting your own name where appropriate. Or you might write a prayer back to the Lord, responding to whatever He has laid on your heart. You could also consider using the space as a Gratitude Journal, recording several things you are thankful for each day. This does wonders redirecting our hearts to the Lord instead of focusing on the difficulties of the day. However you choose to use the space, I pray it will be a meaningful way of spending extra time with Jesus.

I pray *Love, God* will encourage you to grow in your time with the Lord. And that you will find in Him a true and faithful Friend who loves you deeply and is calling you by name.

~ *Day 1* ~

Just a Sigh - from Psalm 5

"Listen to my words, LORD;
consider my sighing."
Psalm 5:1 CSB

When you cannot even find the words, My child, I hear your sigh. That breath exhaled in exasperation, frustration, or exhaustion; words choked out by tears… I hear them all.

And here's the most beautiful part – My Spirit in you does more than just listen. He, Himself, is praying for you with groans that cannot be expressed in mere words. They rise from the depths of your aching heart; then lift directly to My throne in Heaven.

So it's okay to come to Me and just be still. Let My Spirit speak in and for you. He not only knows and understands just how you're thinking and feeling, but He also knows My will for you. So His prayer for you will be exactly what's best. And I will say yes to Him because We are one.

Your sigh, My quiet one, is not empty or wasted breath. And it does not go unheard. Instead, it is a sign to Me that you have surrendered your own will, yielding to Mine. That you recognize your deep need and are reaching out for My hand.

After all, prayer isn't finding just the right words to move My heart. Prayer is baring your soul before Me, then listening to My heart's desire for you. It's hearing the voice of your Shepherd through that same Spirit who is interceding on your behalf.

I love to hear your words, My child. For I am the one who gave you your voice. But when the words won't come, do not despair. Bring to Me whatever you have, even when it's just a sigh. And know that I hear you.

~ Digging Deeper ~

Psalm 5:1-3, Psalm 55:22, Ecclesiastes 5:2, Romans 8:26-27, Philippians 4:6-7, Hebrews 7:24-25, 1 Peter 5:7

~ Questions to Consider ~

Where or how do you see God's love for you in today's Bible passages?

What else did you learn or were you reminded about God today?

Did you learn anything new about yourself or people in general from these passages?

~ **Personal Reflection** ~

Are there things on your heart today that are too painful even to put into words? Do you believe God truly cares about those things?

What promises from Scripture can you claim to be assured of God's care for you? (hint – see list above)

Have you ever imagined what the Holy Spirit might be saying on your behalf? What might you ask Him to say? (And perhaps in just thinking it, you did.)

~ Room to Respond ~

_____

_____

_____

_____

_____

_____

_____

_____

_____

_____

~ Day 2 ~

Hand in Hand – from Psalm 18

"…Your right hand has held me up,
Your gentleness has made me great."
Psalm 18:35 NKJV

From the time you were very little you've fought for independence. The world has taught you to grasp that independence tightly (more so than to Me). To fight for it fiercely. To be self-sufficient. To stand on your own two feet.

Your parents and grandparents clapped, and cheered, and took dozens of pictures the day you toddled clumsily into your first self-reliant steps. They celebrated as you pedaled your first bicycle, swerving all on your own. And your first day of school when you let go of their hand, stepping confidently onto the big, yellow bus…

You'll do the same with your own little ones because you've grown up in a community that lavishly celebrates independence.

But child, that is not My desire for you. Yes, I want you to be strong. But the difference is I want your strength to be in Me. To find that in your moments of weakness, My strength shines brightest as you lean on Me.

As your loving Heavenly Father, I often reach for your hand no matter how little you think you need it. That's because I can see the stumbling blocks much further down the road. And even the wayward roots along your path, invisibly threatening to entangle you.

When you're holding My hand, I'll either keep you from falling, or be right there to help you up if you do. I'm always there hoping you'll take hold. Hoping you'll reach up.

You see, child, My heart's desire is that you would always depend on Me. Every moment. Every day.

Yes, I want you to grow and mature in your faith. To be strong in the convictions you've gained from My Word. And to be bold in going out into the world to be the salt and light I've called you to be.

But child, do it *with* Me. Go there with Me, hand in hand. Let's do life together.

It always works so much better that way.

~ Digging Deeper ~

Psalm 18, Exodus 16:11-21, Psalm 63:7-8, Psalm 73:23, Psalm 139:9-10, Isaiah 41:13, Matthew 6:9-13, 2 Corinthians 12:7-10, Ephesians 6:10

~ Questions to Consider ~

Where or how do you see God's love for you in today's Bible passages?

What else did you learn or were you reminded about God today?

Did you learn anything new about yourself or people in general from these passages?

~ **Personal Reflection** ~

Do you have any memories of walking hand in hand with anyone as a child? Perhaps a parent or grandparent? Or even an older sibling? How did you feel when holding their hand?

Where would you rank yourself on the independence scale? Fiercely independent? I like a little help now and then? I recognize my weaknesses and readily ask for help?

Has it been important to you that others view you as being independent? Why? Have you ever considered that, in some respects, independence may not be the best thing?

In both the Exodus 16 and Matthew 6 passages above, what does God want us to learn about depending on Him? How often do we need Him to help us?

What is it that you're trying to do in your own strength today?

~ **Room to Respond** ~

Consider a prayer of surrender, handing over to the Lord those things to which you're so stubbornly clinging.

_____

_____

_____

_____

_____

_____

_____

_____

_____

_____

_____

~ Room to Respond ~

_____

_____

_____

_____

_____

_____

_____

_____

_____

_____

~ *Day 3* ~

It's Not Hide and Seek – from Acts 7

"but the Most High does not dwell
in sanctuaries made with hands…"
Acts 7:48 CSB

I see you, My child, for I am El Roi. I know you need some guidance and direction, some grace and forgiveness, mercy, love and acceptance. And you already know you can find those things in Me. You need *Me*.

But where, child, are you looking?

If you're hoping to find Me in a place – maybe a church, or gathering of believers, I am there. But perhaps not in the way you might think.

You see, it was never My desire to be kept in a box. Big or small. The God of the universe cannot be contained in things made by human hands.

When King David desired to build a temple for Me, he wanted to honor Me. But his way was the worldly way. For thousands of years, people have built temples for their gods – places they could go to worship and feel closer to them.

But that's not who I am. I AM the God who desires to dwell in the hearts of those who love and follow Me. So when you become My child, you need not search for Me any further than within your own skin. I'm right here already. Always with you.

Just be still for a moment and know I am here.

My Spirit is within you, and My word is already in your heart. You don't have to storm your way to Heaven's gate to find Me. I'm already right here with you and in you!

I am also in the hearts of those with whom you gather for worship. Have you ever noticed how quickly your heart connects with theirs? That's because you share the same spirit. My Spirit. So when you need a little extra encouragement or grace, you can also find Me in them.

Reach out, My child. Allow that brother or sister in faith the privilege of ministering hope and grace to you from the overflow of My Spirit within them. It is a joy, not a burden, to share My love and hope with others. So don't hesitate to be vulnerable and lean on that fellow believer for strength from Me. I will use them to minister to you.

And in the same way, I will use you to be My joy and peace for others out of the overflow from within you.

Are you feeling filled today? Full enough to spill a little of Me on others?

If not, come away with Me. For I've already promised that if you seek Me you will find Me when you seek with all your heart.

Actually, come anyway, full or not. I greatly delight in providing the overflow!

~ **Digging Deeper** ~

Acts 7:46-50, Genesis 16:6-13, Deuteronomy 4:29, 2 Samuel 7:1-7, Psalm 46:10, Jeremiah 29:12-13, John 15:4-8, Acts 17:24, Romans 15:13, Deuteronomy 30:14/Rom 10:6-8

~ **Questions to Consider** ~

Where or how do you see God's love for you in today's Bible passages?

What else did you learn or were you reminded about God today?

Did you learn anything new about yourself or people in general from these passages?

~ **Personal Reflection** ~

Do you ever feel like it's hard to see or feel the presence of God in your life? What are the circumstances surrounding those feelings?

When you are having difficulty feeling God's presence, what can you do to be more aware of the Spirit's presence within you?

Have you invited the Spirit's presence into your life by surrendering your heart to God? If not, please read Giving Your Life to Jesus in the Appendix.

~ Room to Respond ~

_____

_____

_____

_____

_____

_____

_____

_____

_____

_____

_____

_____

_____

_____

~ Room to Respond ~

~ Day 4 ~

...and Justice for All – from Psalm 7

"Arise, O Lord, in anger! Stand up against the fury of my enemies!
Wake up, my God, and bring justice! God is an honest judge."
Psalm 7:6,11 NLT

My child, I'm sure this will be hard to hear, and even harder to understand. But sometimes justice must be delayed because what seems fair isn't always what's best. At least not right now.

I know things have been said and done to you that truly are not fair. I also know you're patiently waiting for Me to be the just and righteous God you know Me to be.

But I need you to understand, child, that justice delayed is not necessarily justice denied. I have not overlooked your trials. Nor am I unmoved by them. It's just that I'm working on a much higher plane where more is involved than you could possibly understand.

I have not forgotten you. I couldn't. You are forever etched into My very being, inscribed on the palm of My hand right next to the scars of My faithful love for you.

So please know that I am at work on your behalf, even though you can't see it just yet. Someday you will, when it's just the right time.

I'm asking you, child, to leave vengeance in My hands. I will repay. I promise.

But there's one more thing you must remember about Me. I am also a merciful God to those who turn from the wrong they've done. I was merciful to you in sending My Son to pay for your sin. Do you remember that moment you realized My grace included you? Can you be happy when My mercy also falls on those who've wronged you?

There are three things you, My child, can do to make Me truly happy - do what is right, love mercy, and walk humbly with Me. And when mercy seems to cancel out what is just and right, then humility will help you yield to My gracious will. I want to assure you again that My plan will always bring about the very best for you. I'm sure that's hard to believe right now. And that's where faith comes in.

Will you trust Me, child, to do what's right and good for everyone... including you? I can do no less.

~ Digging Deeper ~

Psalm 7, Deuteronomy 29:29, Psalm 48:9-11, Psalm 58 (especially verse 11), Isaiah 40:27-31, Isaiah 49:15-16, Isaiah 55:8-11, Micah 6:8, Romans 12:18-21, Ephesians 4:31-32, Philippians 2:1-8, 1 Peter 2:21-25

~ Questions to Consider ~

Where or how do you see God's love for you in today's Bible passages?

What else did you learn or were you reminded about God today?

Did you learn anything new about yourself or people in general from these passages?

~ **Personal Reflection** ~

Have you ever been on the receiving end of injustice? What were the circumstances that seemed unfair?

Has there ever been a point when you wondered if God had lost sight of you?

How might you feel if God grants mercy rather than vengeance to those who've hurt you?

Is there a connection between God's mercy and our need to forgive? How can you forgive what seems unforgiveable?

~ Room to Respond ~

~ Room to Respond ~

_____

_____

_____

_____

_____

_____

_____

_____

_____

_____

_____

_____

_____

_____

_____

~ Day 5 ~

Be Still - from Psalm 46

"Be still, and know that I am God..."
Psalm 46:10 NLT

Do you know what it looks like, what it feels like to really be still, My child? Like actually staying in one place long enough to breathe deeply and listen carefully. And not be surrounded by all the distractions this world might throw at you.

Maybe it's not just worldly interruptions keeping the stillness at bay. Maybe today it feels like everything is falling apart; like the world is crumbling all around you, shaking you to the core. Perhaps walls are closing in, or floors are giving way.

It's nearly impossible to be still when there's chaos all around.

But, My child, that's precisely the time when you are most in need of My stillness.

So picture this with Me - imagine a shimmering city of gold with streams of clear, cool water meandering peacefully through. Are you there with Me? Lush, green trees and blossoming flowers of every possible hue decorate those waterways. And their gentle cascades soothe the turbulence of your troubled soul, leaving only joy as a salve for your sorrow.

Now look a little closer, child. There…in the very center of that city. Someone is sitting on a magnificent throne surrounded by those who worship and adore Him. Those are His children. And each feels as if they are the only one sitting at His feet. That's just how special He makes them feel.

Do you see it, child? Do you see *Me*? I am the one in the midst of that city. Just as I am in you.

So set aside all your worries and cares. In fact, cast them all on Me. Lay down your concerns, your anger, your frustration, even your busyness. Leave them in My capable hands. And just be still.

Now, being still requires trust.

It doesn't mean the world around you will stop spinning. It means that in this moment, you remember who I am - that I am God…your place of refuge. Your source of strength. The one who is always, always, always here for you, especially in the midst of your mess.

Turn your eyes to Me, child. Remember I can handle whatever circumstances are swirling around you. Surrender it all to Me, sinking into the safety of My wings. And just be still because I am God.

~ Digging Deeper ~

Psalm 46:1-11, Psalm 23:1-3, Matthew 11:28-30, Philippians 4:6-7, 1 Peter 5:7

~ Questions to Consider ~

Where or how do you see God's love for you in today's Bible passages?

What else did you learn or were you reminded about God today?

Did you learn anything new about yourself or people in general from these passages?

~ **Personal Reflection** ~

When was the last time you were really still?

Do you like stillness? Or do you have a tendency to fill that space with to-do lists and distractions?

Does stillness necessarily mean quiet? If you struggle with silence, are there ways to be still that might not require absolute silence?

Have you considered building quiet/still time into your schedule so you can get to know your Shepherd even better? Where, when, and how might you do that?

How could reminding yourself of who God is help you be still, even in a world that is not?

~ Room to Respond ~

~ Room to Respond ~

_____

_____

_____

_____

_____

_____

_____

_____

_____

_____

_____

~ Day 6 ~

Bloodstained White – from Hebrews 9

*"he entered the most holy place once for all time,
not by the blood of goats and calves, but by his own blood,
having obtained eternal redemption."*
Hebrews 9:12 CSB

*"…They washed their robes and made them white
in the blood of the Lamb." Revelation 7:14 CSB*

Imagine, child, that you're preparing dinner one evening and the knife – you know the one, extra sharp to cut through carrots like it's cutting butter - that knife slips and slices your thumb. There's blood everywhere! It's on the kitchen counter, in the sink, pooled on the floor… and has splattered your favorite shirt.

In your rush to the doctor, you don't take time to wash out the blood. And hours later, as your newly-stitched thumb still throbs with pain, you remember the shirt, the stains, and the likelihood the bloodstain will never come out. Your favorite shirt is probably ruined because of the blood.

But did you know not all blood is the same?

When human blood mixes with divine, something extraordinary happens. Rather than staining whatever it touches, God-man blood has a cleansing quality. And when it's sprinkled on a sin-stained heart, rather than being ruined, it's washed white as snow.

Repentant hearts are made new because of the blood.

And here's something that may blow your mind – only one person in the universe has blood like that, My Son Jesus. So it seems there would be a limited supply. But because His blood is divine, it's powerful enough to wash every heart that surrenders to Him. His blood and it's sin-cleansing power will never run out.

Have you ever wondered, child, why the Bible is such a bloody book? What's the reason for all that blood anyway? You live in an age of grace where animal sacrifice is no longer required to cover your sin. But reading My Word, you see there was a time when My people had to kill an animal every time they sinned. The animals' blood had to be spilt. And sometimes the priest would dip a hyssop branch in the blood then splatter it on the people gathered around.

Such gruesome sights and smells were purposeful. I intended for My people to hate sin and its consequences. I hoped they would think twice before making a choice that would lead to death. And yet, so often pride would win out, or selfishness, greed or lust, envy or anger. And My people would have to be reminded again that sin leads to death.

That truth has not changed.

But then…at just the right time, My Son Jesus took on human flesh to forever end the need for animal sacrifice. You see, all that blood from centuries of slaughtered animals could never fully wash sin away. It only covered it up until the ultimate sacrifice was made the day My Son's blood ran down that cruel cross. His blood was the only perfect, human blood – the very substance needed to forever pay sins exacting price.

Aren't you glad, child, that you no longer have to watch an animal die to pay for your sin? And aren't you even more thrilled to know your sins can be forever washed away by the perfect blood of Jesus? His blood will never leave a stain. Instead, it has removed the mark of sin on your heart, replacing it with the seal of His Spirit.

Each time you celebrate the Lord's Table (the Eucharist), remember My Son, and the cleansing blood He shed for you. It's the only blood that doesn't stain but whitens.

~ Digging Deeper ~

Hebrews 9:11-28, Psalm 51:7-10, Romans 6:23, 2 Corinthians 5:17, Hebrews 10:1-22, 1 Peter 1:1-2, 1 John 1:7, Revelation 7:9-14

~ Questions to Consider ~

Where or how do you see God's love for you in today's Bible passages?

What else did you learn or were you reminded about God today?

Did you learn anything new about yourself or people in general from these passages?

~ **Personal Reflection** ~

How might you view your sin differently after being reminded of the sacrifices required in the Old Testament, and ultimately Jesus' sacrifice for you?

Have you made that decision to acknowledge Jesus' sacrifice as the payment for your own sin? If so, what prompted that choice? And how does it feel to be washed by the blood of Jesus?

And if not, please read the "Giving Your Life to Jesus" section in the appendix, and consider finally surrendering this very day.

~ Room to Respond ~

~ Room to Respond ~

_____

_____

_____

_____

_____

_____

_____

_____

_____

_____

_____

_____

_____

~ *Day 7* ~

A Champion in Your Corner – from Psalm 43

*"Vindicate me, God, and champion my cause…
Rescue me from the deceitful and unjust person."*
Psalm 43:1 CSB

Could you use a champion in your corner right about now? Someone to fight for you? Defend you?

Since you are My child, you needn't look any further than within.

Not that *you* have the needed strength or wisdom on your own. But you have something even better. Or rather Someone.

I am that Champion in your corner!

My Spirit within you is already at work on your behalf engaging the enemy with My powerful right hand. It's the same hand that parted the sea, shut the mouths of lions, calmed raging storms, and even raised the dead back to life.

That same power is at work in you and for you. So don't be anxious or afraid. I see what you're going through. And I'm here to help.

I realize, child, it may feel like you're all alone in this battle. Like I've forgotten you. Abandoned you. But that's just not true.

I'm here to lead you to victory!

So keep trusting Me. My Spirit is with you lighting the way. His truth will guide you to a place of safety and rest…at just the right time.

But as you wait for that respite, stay closely connected to Me. Did you know the word "hope" in My Word literally means to be tied to something? Connected?

So hope in Me, My child. Trust that I am exactly who I say I am, and I can do what I've said I can do.

And that includes bringing you joy even in the midst of your battle. How can that be? It happens when your absolute trust in Me moves your eyes away from the battle, and to My face, instead.

When you see the love and strength I have for you there, you will not be able to contain the joy. You will be reminded just how much you mean to Me. And the promises in My Word will flood your heart and soul with an unexplainable peace.

And while you're there, lost in My gaze, I will be in your corner fighting that battle for you. There's no one greater or stronger to fight on your behalf.   Not even you.

Let me have this one, child. And the next one, too. Because I love you.

~ Digging Deeper ~

Psalm 43, Exodus 14:13-14, Deuteronomy 3:21-22, Deuteronomy 20:1-4, 2 Chronicles 20:13-23, Psalm 34:15-19, Psalm 60:11-12, Isaiah 41:10, Romans 8:31-37, Romans 15:13

~ Questions to Consider ~

Where or how do you see God's love for you in today's Bible passages?

What else did you learn or were you reminded about God today?

Did you learn anything new about yourself or people in general from these passages?

~ **Personal Reflection** ~

What battle are you facing today? Do you feel like you have anyone helpful in your corner?

Have you asked the Lord for help? Or have you been trying to fight on your own?

It's true that God sometimes fights our battles for us. But sometimes He asks us to engage, then gives us the strength to do so. How can we know when to fight, and when to stand down and let Him do it for us?

Have you ever experienced God taking control of a battle for you?

Describe that experience, and remember to thank Him for His faithfulness.

~ Room to Respond ~

~ Room to Respond ~

_____

_____

_____

_____

_____

_____

_____

_____

_____

_____

_____

_____

_____

~ *Day 8* ~

Confident! – from Psalm 27

"The LORD is my light and my salvation - so why should I be afraid?
The LORD is my fortress, protecting me from danger,
so why should I tremble? Though a mighty army surrounds me,
my heart will not be afraid...I will remain confident."
Psalm 27:1,3 NLT

My child, would you say you feel confident? I see your heart and know this is often a struggle for you.

You look around at others and feel like you don't quite measure up to them, or to their expectations of you.

You look at your situation and are completely overwhelmed. You feel inadequate, unqualified, ill-equipped, unprepared.

You look in the mirror and find failure: so much less than what you had expected of yourself.

And you look in My Word, seeing only how far short of My holiness you fall.

You forget you are dust.

But I don't.

Let's try this instead, child - rather than finding confidence in your own achievements, try finding it in Me. I will never let you down. It will be My great delight to be the one who lights your way, covers you in My redeeming blood, and stands strong to face your enemies. I will be faithful to complete what I have begun. And I have begun a good thing in and through you!

I have gifted you with strengths and abilities that are perfectly suited to My plans for you. And I have already promised to provide everything you need to accomplish all I've called you to do.

And keep this in mind, child – it's not up to you to work out all the details and make sure everything is completed. That's My job.

And I'm up to it.

You, on the other hand, were never meant to shoulder that responsibility. Your job is to stay close to Me, to follow Me each and every day. To step in the footprints I've left for you, to walk through doors I open, and take advantage of opportunities I place in your path.

Now, don't be surprised, child, when those opportunities occasionally look more like interruptions or obstacles. Don't let that deter or frustrate you. Don't let it steal your confidence. Have confidence in Me, and in My ability to work it all out for your good and My glory. It's what I do best.

~ Digging Deeper ~

Psalm 27, Psalm 71:1-8, Romans 8:28, 1 Corinthians 12:7&11, 2 Corinthians 9:8, 2 Corinthians 12:9, Philippians 1:6, 2 Peter 1:3

~ Questions to Consider ~

Where or how do you see God's love for you in today's Bible passages?

What else did you learn or were you reminded about God today?

Did you learn anything new about yourself or people in general from these passages?

~ **Personal Reflection** ~

How would you describe your level of confidence? Do you tend to place the burden of success on yourself?

In what circumstances do you tend to lack confidence? Work, family, among friends?

What has caused you to lose confidence in the past?

What might it look like to find confidence in God and His ability to work out the details of your life? Have there been times in your past when you've seen Him come through for you?

How might it change your daily challenges to know that God has promised to finish what He starts?

~ Room to Respond ~

~ Room to Respond ~

_____

_____

_____

_____

_____

_____

_____

_____

_____

_____

_____

_____

_____

_____

~ Day 9 ~

Beyond the Stars – from Psalm 121

"I lift my eyes toward the mountains. Where will my help come from?
My help comes from the Lord, the Maker of heaven and earth."
Psalm 121:1-2 CSB

My child, you are weary and worn. Frustrated and angry. Hurt and afraid. But do you realize you've looked everywhere for help except to Me?

You've even looked up; but haven't made it past the stars.

Have you considered who put them there, and why? Have you thought about who formed the mountains, strong and immovable? Or have you stood by the ocean with the waves licking your feet, and noted that something holds them there within some unseen boundary?

That something is Me, child! I am the Creator and sustainer of the universe, of all that is grand and glorious. I tell the mountain to stand firm and tall as it reaches for the sky. And to the ocean waves I say, "You may come this far, but no farther." I hold it all within My ever-capable hands.

And at the very same time, I hold your heart.

Not with human hands that may grow weary or frightened, and let go. But ready, steady hands that say, "Take hold of mine, and walk with Me."

Could you use a hand like that today? You'll recognize it's Mine by the deep and rugged, nail-pierced scars.

And if you look close enough, you'll see your name engraved there, too. Never to be erased. When I look down and see the scar, I don't remember the pain. I see your name next to it and know it was worth it all. Just for you.

That same hand is still as long and strong as the day it formed the universe. It has not grown shorter or weaker through the centuries. It is still willing and able to reach yours when you feel like you're falling.

I know it feels, at times, like I've let go. You wonder if maybe I've looked the other way. Or maybe been distracted by the many others slipping and sliding beside you.

But know this, child – I never sleep. I never get distracted. You have My full attention at all times. And what feels like a fall is simply your opportunity to either fly with the strength of My Spirit, or be caught in My waiting, sturdy arms.

I am here at all times to watch over and protect you. If you're waiting for the world, for some other cosmic power or human being to intervene on your behalf, then you have every right to fear the outcome. For in them there are no guarantees.

But in Me…that's where you'll find shelter from all that might harm you. I am here to protect you day and night, wherever you go, in this life and the next.

So look up… past the mountains, and the sky, and the stars. It may sound like a long way. But it isn't really. I'm actually right here with you, just waiting for your gaze to meet Mine. Because I am the Help you need.

Just ask.

~ Digging Deeper ~

Psalm 121, Job 38:4-11, Psalm 46:1-5, Isaiah 49:16, Matthew 7:7, Philippians 4:19

~ Questions to Consider ~

Where or how do you see God's love for you in today's Bible passages?

What else did you learn or were you reminded about God today?

Did you learn anything new about yourself or people in general from these passages?

~ **Personal Reflection** ~

In what areas of your life are you most in need today?

Have you ever wondered if perhaps God has lost sight of you? What were the circumstances?

What does it mean to you that the God of the universe is your Guardian and Protector?

Do you feel you can trust God to "protect you from all harm?" Why or why not? (If you struggle to trust Him, why not use the Room for Reflection below to talk with Him about it.)

~ Room to Respond ~

_____

_____

_____

_____

_____

_____

_____

_____

_____

_____

_____

~ Room to Respond ~

_____

_____

_____

_____

_____

_____

_____

_____

_____

_____

_____

_____

_____

_____

~ *Day 10* ~

Nourishment for the Day – from Jeremiah 15

"Your words were found, and I ate them.
Your words became a delight to me and the joy of my heart,
for I bear your name, LORD God of Armies."
Jeremiah 15:16 NLT

Have you discovered My words, child? I've placed them right in your hands. Take them in. Deeply. Let them become part of you. As you do, you will find they taste like joy on your tongue.

Have you ever tasted joy, My child? It's sweet and pure like honey dripping from the comb.

My words will bring so much joy your face will shine like the Son, and your heart will sing with delight. You will know the melody, My child, for I have been singing it over you like a lullaby since you became one of My own.

And don't forget that you now bear My name. I gave it to you when I adopted you as My very own. Wear it with pride. Let it be your strength and joy, for you are a child of the Lord God of Heaven's Armies.

You are blessed beyond measure!

And I give you My words to remind you just how truly blessed and loved you are. So enjoy a feast of those words as you begin your day. They will be just the nourishment you need for whatever lies ahead.

Oh, and don't forget to share your feast with others!

~ Digging Deeper ~

Jeremiah 15, Psalm 19:9-10, Psalm 119:14-16, Isaiah 40:8, Jeremiah 1:9, Zephaniah 3:17

~ Questions to Consider ~

Where or how do you see God's love for you in today's Bible passages?

What else did you learn or were you reminded about God today?

Did you learn anything new about yourself or people in general from these passages?

~ **Personal Reflection** ~

There are so many ways you could "eat" God's words today. What's your favorite way to take it in – an ink and paper Bible? Bible app? Music? Podcast? Listening to Scripture being read? Why do you prefer that way?

What can you do to help yourself truly ingest more of the Word when you hear or read it?

Is there a particular verse or Bible passage that brings you great joy?

When was the last time you shared what you were reading in God's Word with someone else? (feasts are meant to be shared!) Do you enjoy when others talk with you about what God has been showing them in His Word?

Can you say that you enjoy reading God's Word? If not, what might help? If you do, are you encouraging others to do the same?

~ Room to Respond ~

_____

_____

_____

_____

_____

_____

_____

_____

_____

_____

~ *Day 11* ~

You've Never Been This Way Before – from Joshua 3

"…When you see the Levitical priests carrying the Ark of the Covenant of the LORD your God, move out from your positions and follow them. Since you have never traveled this way before, they will guide you."
Joshua 3:3-4 NLT

Have you sensed that nudge, My child? You know the one… that itch that it's time for something new. Something different. Something other than what you've known before. Something beyond what has become comfortable and safe.

Sometimes that feeling simply comes from being dissatisfied; a lack of contentment in My "stay!"

But other times, that nudge is My Spirit coaxing you outside your comfort zone into courage's corner. That's MY corner. A place where faith and trust can grow. A place where you have opportunities to spread your Spirit-wings and fly into the unknown.

How can you know if the nudge is from Me? Try asking yourself these questions –

Would it cause you to rely more on yourself, or on Me?

Is it something you would choose on your own? Or would it have to be a God-ask for you to consider it?

Who would get the glory from such a change?

My friend, Joshua, took up a challenge from Me many centuries ago. And maybe with the same lack of courage you're currently feeling. Are you a bit unsure? I reminded Joshua time and time again to "be strong and courageous." And that's because he was anxious, needing those reminders.

Even though he had already led My people into battle under Moses' leadership, and with great success, when it came to taking the lead himself, he needed constant reassurance that he was not in it alone.

And neither are you!

Don't miss the fact, My courageous one, that I recognized My children had never been where I was calling them to go. I knew it was a daunting challenge. That's why My presence went before them in the Ark of the Covenant. Though they couldn't see Me, they knew I dwelt with them there.

And now My Spirit dwells in you giving you everything you need to follow Me...and follow through – strength, power, courage, direction. And even peace!

But child, don't overlook the detail that My priests had to first step out in faith before they would see My miracle-working power. I know you want to see proof of My presence in this new venture. But oftentimes proof doesn't come until after you've taken that first obedient step into the unknown.

Are you worried you won't be equipped to handle the new and different? Won't be strong enough? Smart enough? Bold enough?

Enough!

My servant and friend, Moses, Joshua's mentor, felt the very same way. He even went so far as to ask Me to send someone else instead. But I had designed him to be enough...with My help. I supplied all he needed to carry out My new calling for His life.

And I will do the same for you.

Trust Me!

~ Digging Deeper ~

Joshua 3:1-17, Exodus 3:10-14, Exodus 4:10-13, Joshua 1:1-9, Isaiah 43:18-19, John 14:5-6, 2 Corinthians 9:8, Philippians 1:6, Philippians 4:19, Hebrews 13:20-21, 2 Peter 1:3

~ Questions to Consider ~

Where or how do you see God's love for you in today's Bible passages?

What else did you learn or were you reminded about God today?

Did you learn anything new about yourself or people in general from these passages?

~Personal Reflection ~

Do you like change? Why or why not?

Have you sensed a calling, or maybe just a nudge to do something new? Maybe it's as simple as reaching out to someone you never have before.

How might God be trying to stretch you outside your comfort zone?

What do you feel you lack that would make it difficult to answer "yes" to God's call?

What promises can you claim from His Word (see list above) to give you the confidence to step out in faith?

~ Room for Reflection ~

~ Room to Respond ~

_____

_____

_____

_____

_____

_____

_____

_____

_____

_____

_____

_____

_____

~ Day 12 ~

Confession: So Good for the Soul – from Psalm 32

"How joyful is the one whose transgression is forgiven."
Psalm 32:1 CSB

Is there something on your heart, My child? Something that's weighing you down because you have not yet brought it to Me? Some sin that's keeping us at a distance because you haven't found the words, or the courage, or maybe the will to confess?

The first thing I want you to know is that distance isn't on My part. Since you are My child, I have promised never to leave or abandon you. So if some unconfessed sin is keeping you from Me, check to see whether you have moved away. It's not the other way around. And you're welcome to come back, closer to Me, at any time.

But when you do, please come with a heart ready to surrender that sin, that idol, that distraction from Me to which you cling so tightly. As any good father would, I am ready and wanting to forgive. But I won't just look the other way, acting is if nothing is wrong, because that ultimately is not best for you.

What *is* best for you is confession… it's good for the soul.

Acknowledging your sin to Me and no longer trying to hide it will free you from the guilt that has pulled you away from Me. And oh… how I miss you!

And here's the best part – when you've given your heart to Me, your sin is covered by My Son Jesus' blood. I will not charge you with the penalty of that sin because it's already been paid for.

So why confess it? Why bring it up at all? It's for your own sake, child. Have you not noticed that burden on your shoulders as you've carried it's weight all alone? Have you not noticed the guilt that lowers your eyes from Mine?

I have promised not to condemn you once you're Mine. But I will allow sin to do its work of misery, which in turn will nudge you back in My direction.

Do you see Me waiting with open arms? You'll find that always to be true, no matter what you've done, or where you've been. I will always welcome you home.

And the welcome will be so much sweeter once you've cleared the air.Remember the story of the prodigal son? His father was waiting with open arms to welcome him home. But gave him space, as they embraced, to confess that he had sinned. His father already knew. But perhaps he also realized that confession would be an integral part of his healing and restoration. Confession is never fun, My child. It's hard. But it's oh, so freeing!

Maybe we could begin the day again and start with confession.

So…is there something on your heart, My child?

~ Digging Deeper ~

Psalm 32:1-5, Psalm 51, Psalm 139:23-24, Luke 15:11-24, Romans 8:1, Hebrews 12:3-13, Hebrews 13:5

~ Questions to Consider ~

Where or how do you see God's love for you in today's Bible passages?

What else did you learn or were you reminded about God today?

Did you learn anything new about yourself or people in general from these passages?

~ **Personal Reflection** ~

Do you find it easy to say, "I'm sorry?" and ask forgiveness? Or is it difficult for you? and why?

Is there something you've been holding back from talking with God about because you aren't sure if God can/will forgive you?

Do you have children? If yes, how do you feel towards them when they come to you to confess something they've done, and ask forgiveness?

Sometimes when we sin, we suffer for it. What is the difference between punishment and discipline? And what role might natural consequences play when we sin?

If God does discipline us, does He do so out of spite, or love? How do you know? (Hebrews 12:3-13)

~ Room for Reflection ~

_____

_____

_____

_____

_____

_____

_____

_____

_____

_____

_____

_____

_____

_____

~ Room to Respond ~

_____

_____

_____

_____

_____

_____

_____

_____

_____

_____

_____

_____

_____

_____

_____

~ Day 13 ~

Where Are You? – from Genesis 3

*"So the LORD God called out to the man and said to him,
'Where are you?'"*
Genesis 3:9 CSB

Where are you, My child?

Does that seem like a strange question coming from an all-knowing God? It's meant to. Meant to stop you in your tracks and make you think. Because it isn't Me who needs to know. It's you!

Not so much geographically. That you can see just looking around you.

But wait! Look around again… Really look! Where are you? Are you where I've called you to be? Do you even know where that is? Have you asked Me lately? Or have you just let life take you where it wanted without even realizing it?

It's so easy to get drawn away from Me by the things your world offers – pleasure, happiness, love, success, fulfillment. But are they real? Are they lasting?

Apart from Me, the answer is, "No."

But *with* Me, when I'm dwelling with you and you're doing the same with Me… that's where you'll find true and lasting joy, contentment, peace.

You have a very real enemy in this world. He knows exactly where you are right now, too. He's there, just as he was with Eve in the Garden, enticing you to take a step… just one for now, then another, and another away from Me - toward that thing, that place, that person he swears will bring you happiness.

But in reality, he is a thief who wants to steal your peace, kill your joy, and destroy the relationships you cherish most, especially ours. Have you seen him lately? Is he close by?

If you're not really sure where you are right now, this is a good time to look around and be sure it's not near him.

How can you tell, you may ask? Think for a moment — are you closer to Me than you used to be, or further away? Is it easier to hear My voice these days, or harder? Are you drawing others closer to Me, or leading them in another direction?

My desire is that these questions would bring a smile to your face and joy to your heart as you realize how precious you are to Me. And as you recall My many promises to never leave you.

My desire is that the answer comes quickly to your lips, "I'm right here with You, Father. There's no place I'd rather be."

But if the answer is slow in coming, if you're realizing that perhaps there's more distance between us than you had noticed, won't you take a few moments even now to consider how far you've drifted, and scooch a little closer?

Where are you?

I'm asking for a friend. And that friend is you.

~ Digging Deeper ~

Genesis 3:1-24, Psalm 73:28, Psalm 145:18, John 10:10, John 15:1-11, Hebrews 4:16, 7:25, 10:22, 11:6, James 4:8

~ Questions to Consider ~

Where or how do you see God's love for you in today's Bible passages?

What else did you learn or were you reminded about God today?

Did you learn anything new about yourself or people in general from these passages?

~ **Personal Reflection** ~

Do you feel like God is asking where you are this very day? If so, do you know the answer?

How can you know where you are in your relationship with God? Do you believe He can reveal that to you? If so, how might He do that?

Do you regularly spend time with God in prayer and in His Word?

What other spiritual disciplines or practices help you stay close to God?

~ Room to Respond ~

If you're still not really sure where you are, ask the Lord to show you.
He would be happy to.

_____

_____

_____

_____

_____

_____

_____

_____

_____

_____

_____

_____

_____

_____

~ Room to Respond ~

_____

_____

_____

_____

_____

_____

_____

_____

_____

_____

_____

_____

_____

~ Day 14 ~

No More Shame – from Psalm 103

"He forgives all my sins…He has removed our sins
as far from us as the east is from the west."
Psalm 103:3,12 NLT

So child, let's have a conversation about your past sin - that stuff that happened years ago, last month, yesterday…

Oh wait! There's nothing to talk about. You already brought it to Me, asked for forgiveness, and walked away from it.

And when you did that, I forgave you. Completely. So completely that I can't even remember what it was. I blotted it out of your record, tossed it into the deepest part of the sea, removed it from you as far as the east is from the west. Have you ever considered how far apart those are, My child? They never meet! I will never again remind you of past sin that we've already taken care of together.

But that doesn't mean your enemy won't try to use it against you. Or you might even find yourself dredging those things up in the quiet of your own heart.

When that happens, child, remind yourself that there is no more condemnation for My children who've brought it to Me. It's not My desire to shame you. You are forgiven. And your sin is forgotten. I choose to remember it no more.

I love you so much! And My desire is that you would live in the freedom of My grace. And that includes freedom from the shame of past sins.

So child, since we can't really talk about old sins, let's talk about blessings instead. Maybe you could start with freedom. Let Me help get you started -

Freedom from the chains of sin
Freedom from comparison
Freedom to trust again
Freedom to love deeply

Freedom to forgive others

Freedom to be vulnerable

There are so many more. Enjoy remembering My goodness to you. It's been My pleasure, and will continue to be.

~ Digging Deeper ~

Psalm 103, Isaiah 43:25, Isaiah 44:22, Romans 7:24-8:2, 1 Corinthians 13:4-5, Galatians 5:1, Colossians 2:13-14, 1 John 3:19-22

~ Questions to Consider ~

Where or how do you see God's love for you in today's Bible passages?

What else did you learn or were you reminded about God today?

Did you learn anything new about yourself or people in general from these passages?

~ **Personal Reflection** ~

Do you struggle with past sins haunting you?

Have you talked with Jesus about them, confessed them to Him and asked for forgiveness?

Did you know of His many promises to forget our sins?

How should His forgiveness of our sins reflect in our forgiveness of others?

What freedoms can you add to the list above?

~ Room to Respond ~

~ Room to Respond ~

_____

_____

_____

_____

_____

_____

_____

_____

_____

_____

_____

_____

_____

_____

~ *Day 15* ~

I Am Your Deliverance – from Psalm 35

*"Draw the spear and javelin against my pursuers,
and assure me, 'I am your deliverance.'"*
Psalm 35:3 CSB

Don't be afraid, My child.

I hear you crying out for deliverance. I see the enemy pursuing you - weapons drawn, ready to tear you down the moment I lose sight of you.

But that will never happen, My frightened one.

Never will there come a day, not even a moment when My eyes are not on you or My wings fail to overspread you.

Never.

I am here for you, even when you cannot see Me.

And here's a secret, child… your enemy Satan *can* see Me. He knows I am fighting for you. And it has him trembling. He may continue to roar as he prowls ever closer. But he can only get as close as I allow.

Have you ever noticed how the waves of the sea come crashing to shore, but go no further? Do you know what holds them back? Do you know *Who* holds them back? I tell them they may "toss and roar, but they can never pass the boundaries I set."*

And I do the same for you.

Now I know, My anxious one, there are times you feel like rescue is too long coming. You ask, "Lord, how long will you look on," as if I have forgotten your pain or peril. You fear I've lost sight of you. Or even worse, that I just don't care enough, or am powerless to deliver you from the evil one.

But child, I see it. I know it. I feel it, for My Spirit is within you. And we will not abandon you.

Look up and see, for even now I'm rising up from My throne to defend you. I will be a shield between you and the enemy. And I will strike a blow against him that reminds him just how precious you are to

Me. He'd better remember that next time because I am for you!

And if I am for you, who can stand against you? It is, after all, My joy and privilege as your Heavenly Father to take good care of you. Your well-being is My responsibility, and I will not neglect that.

I know the enemy is close. And loud. But he can only roar. He cannot bite those who are most precious to Me. And child, that is you.

Once you see how I have delivered you, be sure to share the news with others. They, too, need to know how much I love and want to care for them.

So sing it out, loud and long… "I am your deliverance."

~ Digging Deeper ~

Psalm 35, *Psalm 35:17, Jeremiah 5:22, Mark 9:24, Romans 8:31

~ Questions to Consider ~

Where or how do you see God's love for you in today's Bible passages?

What else did you learn or were you reminded about God today?

Did you learn anything new about yourself or people in general from these passages?

~Personal Reflection ~

Are you in need of deliverance today? Maybe it's from doubt, or fear, pain, or even yourself. Name the enemy that is pursuing you.

How have you seen God deliver you in the past?

If you cannot recall any, have you seen Him deliver someone else? Do you believe He can do the same for you?

Do you believe He will? Why or why not?

~ Room for Reflection ~

If you're struggling to believe that God will rescue you, look at the father in Mark 9:24. How did he feel about what Jesus might do for his son? If you feel the same way, you can use this space to talk to Him about it.

_____

_____

_____

_____

_____

_____

_____

_____

_____

_____

_____

_____

~ Room to Respond ~

_____

_____

_____

_____

_____

_____

_____

_____

_____

_____

_____

_____

_____

_____

~ Day 16 ~

I'm Listening – from Psalm 17

*"Hear me, LORD…listen to my cry.
Hear my prayer—"
Psalm 17:1 NIV*

I'm listening, My child. I hear your sorrows and concerns, your fears and frustrations – even those you will not…cannot say aloud. Just like a father tenderly kneels to hear the plaintive whispers of his wounded child, I too bend low to hear the cries of your heart.

You see, child, I've looked closely into that heart of yours - that sometimes stubborn, occasionally fickle, and often fearful heart. But here's the thing: I have tested it and found it pure and clean before Me. Not necessarily because of what you've done or thought. But because My Son has made it clean with His own precious blood. So when I look at you, I see His goodness, and righteousness, and faithfulness and declare you clean through Him. When I look into your heart, I see nothing to condemn.

His sacrifice has changed your heart, helping you choose the right path. My path. And His Spirit enables you to do what is humanly impossible, as you firmly resolve to keep your thoughts and actions pure, daily yielding them to Me.

And that clears the way for Me to act on your behalf.

Remember, child, the many times I have answered you before. It gives Me great delight to do so! You are learning you can come to Me, knowing I will listen intently and answer graciously because of My deep and abiding love for you. After all, My child, you are the very apple of My eye.

When your wounded heart needs a safe place to hide, My wings will spread wide to shelter you. When you feel the enemy closing in, I will rise up like a mother bear to protect you. There is nothing more powerful than My presence. And I have promised never to leave or forsake you.

Never. Ever.

So come, my child. Bring your cares to Me, knowing I will listen and help. Find in Me that certain peace and contentment that only I can give.

But here is the challenge, dear one: find that satisfaction in Me. Simply in being *with* Me. Not in getting the answer you are seeking. Not in seeing all the swirling circumstances suddenly set right. But opening your eyes each morning to see that I'm still here right beside you, ready to walk today's path with you. Or rather, ready to take you by the hand and lead you down Mine, if you're willing.

Are you? Do you trust Me? Let's see...

~ Digging Deeper ~

Psalm 17, Psalm 116:2-4, Romans 8:1, Philippians 4:6-7, Hebrews 13:5, 1 Peter 5:7, 2 Peter 1:3-4

~ Questions to Consider ~

Where or how do you see God's love for you in today's Bible passages?

What else did you learn or were you reminded about God today?

Did you learn anything new about yourself or people in general from these passages?

~ Personal Reflection ~

Do you have someone in your life who you feel really listens to you? Can you tell them everything?

Do you spend time each day sharing your heart with Jesus? Do you feel like He hears you, and cares about what's on your heart?

If Jesus is all you have, could He be to you all that you need? Are there verses you can claim to remind yourself this is true? (see passages above)

~ Room to Respond ~

~ Room to Respond ~

~ *Day 17* ~

Grace Alone – from Acts 15

"Now then, why are you testing God by putting a yoke on the disciples' necks that
neither our ancestors nor we have been able to bear?
On the contrary, we believe that we are saved through the grace
of the Lord Jesus in the same way they are."
Acts 15:10-11 CSB

Stop trying so hard, My child!

Relationship with Me was never meant to be about the rules. Yes, it's good for you to do the right things, following the instructions I have given in My Word. Obedience is My love language after all.

But your obedience should flow naturally from your love for Me; not in an attempt to gain My approval. It should be the result of our relationship. It doesn't produce it.

You see, child, anything you DO to try to add to My gift of grace actually takes something away from it. A gift isn't really a gift if it demands something in return.

My Son's death on the cross paid your sin-debt in full. There is nothing more required for your adoption into My family. Jesus paid it all!

So if you're somehow feeling unworthy of such a gift, like there's something more you must do to earn the right to belong to Me… Child, that is the message of your enemy and mine, the devil. He seeks to weigh you down beneath a burden of guilt and shame. He wants you working so hard to receive My favor and earn a place in Heaven with Me that you miss the completeness of grace.

People, usually religious people, have been saying for centuries that there is more to be done to be part of My family. Rituals to perform. Sacrifices to make in an attempt to be worthy.

But please hear Me say this – there is nothing more you must do to be My child than to accept, by faith, the redeeming grace and forgiveness My Son already paid for. It is a gift you must take. I won't force it on anyone. And anyone who accepts it must do so acknowledging their desperate need. But in the end, it is a free gift.

The only thing I ask in return is your surrendered heart. Love Me. Follow Me. Make Me Lord of your life. I have earned that.

All those other things you feel you should do, or someone else is telling you that you should - those are not necessarily bad things. But please do them out of your love for Me and appreciation for what My Son Jesus did for you. Then those acts of kindness and mercy will indeed please Me.

Child, salvation was never meant to be an extra burden you must bear. It's meant to lift the burden of perfection from off your shoulders, and place it squarely on Jesus'. His are able to bear what yours cannot. And He is more than happy to do so.

So stop trying so hard to gain My love. You already have it. Now simply live in and through it.

~ Digging Deeper ~

Acts 15:1-11, John 14:15, 23-24, Galatians 5:4-6, Ephesians 2:8-10, 2 Timothy 1:9-12, Titus 3:5, 1 John 5:2-4

~ Questions to Consider ~

Where or how do you see God's love for you in today's Bible passages?

What else did you learn or were you reminded about God today?

Did you learn anything new about yourself or people in general from these passages?

~ **Personal Reflection** ~

Have you received God's free gift of redemption through the grace of His Son Jesus? If not, please see Giving Your Life to Jesus in the back of this book.

If you are a child of God, has anyone tried to convince you that there is more you must do to gain God's favor or secure a home in Heaven some day?

What can we do to add to our chances of getting into Heaven when we die? (I hope your answer is "nothing!")

How does it feel to know that your eternal destiny does not depend on how "good" you are, but instead on how gracious God is? What does that mean to you?

~ Room to Respond ~

Consider writing a prayer of gratitude for God's gift of grace

~ Room to Respond ~

_____

_____

_____

_____

_____

_____

_____

_____

_____

_____

_____

_____

~ *Day 18* ~

Betrayed! – from Psalm 41

"Even my best friend, the one I trusted completely,
the one who shared my food, has turned against me."
Psalm 41:9 NLT

Oh, how it stings!

Child, believe Me. I know just how it feels to have a friend betray you. It happened to Me too, when Judas kissed My cheek then stepped aside for My captors to take Me away. He used our friendship against Me, knowing just where I would be when I needed comfort and peace. He knew I would go to the Garden. And he brought My enemies there.

So yes, child. I know the sting.

I heard what they said and know what they did to you. I know how deeply you've been wounded. And I'm here to put My arm around you and pull you in close.

Can you feel it? Will you choose to feel My love more deeply than you feel the pain?

Will you choose to focus on My face instead of recalling the one that hurt you?

You will surely be tempted, My child, to rehearse the betrayal over and over again. You will seek answers to questions you were never given the chance to ask. You will wonder what you might have done to cause it. What you might have done to prevent it.

But in the end, those questions will only leave you sad, discouraged, and perhaps even angry. The enemy will encourage you to remain there in your bitterness and despair.

I have a much better suggestion – bring it to Me. Come to Me in your weariness and heartache. Let Me take that burden from you.

How can I do that? By offering you My peace.

The peace I give is like nothing else you've known. It's beyond anything you could possibly understand. And yet, it's as real as the pain it can replace…if you'll let it. If you'll let Me.

I can pick up the broken pieces and make them into something brand new.

I can set you free from the chains of heartache, and comfort you as you mourn the loss of what once was. I can take the ashes of your loss and melt them into a crown of beauty. And I can dress you in the splendor of My majesty.

What do you say? Are you ready to take Me at My word and let Me lift you up above it all?

Then those who betrayed you will only be able to look on and wonder how you manage to still have joy.

And know this, child – I will not let them go unpunished. I am Justice! I will repay when the time is right. Trust Me to handle this in the best way, at the best time. That's what I do. And I will do it for you because I love you, and you are Mine.

I am the friend who will never let you down.

~ Digging Deeper ~

Psalm 41:5-12, Psalm 55:12-16, Proverbs 18:24, Isaiah 61:1-3, Micah 7:5-8, Matthew 11:28-30, Mark 14:43-46, John 13:21-30, John 14:27, Philippians 4:6-7

~ Questions to Consider ~

Where or how do you see God's love for you in today's Bible passages?

What else did you learn or were you reminded about God today?

Did you learn anything new about yourself or people in general from these passages?

~ **Personal Reflection**

Have you ever been betrayed by a friend? Has someone close to you said or done something that deeply hurt you?

What can you do, even this very day, to help lessen that sting – or allow Jesus to do so? Do you believe that Jesus can help you? What step might you take in that direction?

Have past hurts made it more difficult to develop close relationships?

What might help when it comes to opening your heart to new friends?

Have you ever been the one to betray another? What steps could you take to restore that relationship?

~ Room for Reflection ~

~ Room to Respond ~

_____

_____

_____

_____

_____

_____

_____

_____

_____

_____

_____

_____

_____

_____

~ *Day 19* ~

Tears – from Psalm 6

*"I am weary from my groaning;
with my tears I dampen my bed and drench my couch every night.
My eyes are swollen from grief...the Lord has heard
the sound of my weeping. The Lord has heard my plea for help;
the Lord accepts my prayer."*
Psalm 6:6-9 CSB

Did you know, child, that one day there will be no more need for tears. There will be no more sorrow or crying, for I will wipe away every last tear. But that won't happen until you've joined Me here in Heaven.

In the meantime, life on Earth is no longer perfect, as I created it to be. Sin has cursed your world with brokenness and disease, separation and pain...so many things that bring anguish and tears.

Those tears do not go unnoticed, My child. I see each one and the circumstances behind them. My heart breaks with yours. I even collect each of those tears in a bottle so you'll know just how much I care that you're hurting.

I know at times it feels like the tears may never end, like things will never be the same again. But listen, child, as I whisper words of hope and comfort deep into your soul. You don't have to wait till Heaven for Me to wipe those tears. I can do so even now. Do you feel My tender hand on your tear-stained cheek, brushing away each tear that falls?

Bring those tears to Me, child. I care. And no one can help you like I can.

You see, I know what tomorrow holds. I know how this will end. And when. And I'm here to walk beside you till that time comes, and forever after. My Spirit within you wants to permeate your soul with My peace. He's there to reassure your heart that I'm working even now on your behalf to be sure this all turns out right.

You don't need to hide those tears from Me, child. After all, I created them. Let Me help you process them and in time, when you're ready, move ahead. I'm here for you. Feel free to cry on My shoulder.

~ Digging Deeper ~

Psalm 6, Psalm 56:8, Psalm 126:5, Jeremiah 29:11, Romans 8:28, 1
Peter 1:5-9, Revelation 7:17, 21:4

~ Questions to Consider ~

Where or how do you see God's love for you in today's Bible passages?

What else did you learn or were you reminded about God today?

Did you learn anything new about yourself or people in general from
these passages?

~ **Personal Reflection** ~

When was the last time you cried? Do you feel like you have to hide your tears from others? Are you afraid it might make them feel uncomfortable or make you look weak?

How do you think God feels about your tears? Do you think He sees them as weakness, or an opportunity to comfort and encourage you?

How might God be able to help you with your grief or pain? Do you know any promises from His Word that might help you through sad or painful times?

~ Room to Respond ~

_____

_____

_____

_____

_____

_____

_____

_____

_____

_____

_____

_____

_____

~ *Day 20* ~

Still the Resurrection and the Life – from John 11

"Jesus said to her, 'I am the resurrection and the life...'"
John 11:25 CSB

My Friend, and I call you that because that is what you are. You listen to My voice, and you do what I say. That tells Me you trust Me. You believe the instructions I give truly are My best for you so you follow them. And that makes us friends.

So, My friend, does it feel like I'm taking a little too long to answer you? Are you anxious that perhaps I might not come through in time, and things could end up in a place beyond repair?

Do you remember the story of My friends Lazarus, Mary, and Martha? They sent word to Jesus when Lazarus was very sick because they knew two things: that I would care very deeply about their suffering, and that I had the power to change their circumstances.

But *because* I loved them so much, I delayed going to them. Is that truth hard to grasp, dear friend? That I would delay an answer because I love so deeply? Does it seem like the loving thing would be to go to them right away, offer My comfort and peace. And then heal him? Wouldn't *that* be the loving thing to do?

The answer might surprise you because it was "no." Not on that occasion. Remember child, I can see beyond the moment. Beyond the present circumstances. Beyond your pain and fear to what lies ahead...just beyond the valley you're walking through.

So I delayed long enough for what seemed the worst of outcomes. My friend Lazarus died.

His sisters were devastated. So when I the time was right, I went to them. And in the midst of their grief, I reminded them who I am - the Resurrection and the Life. Yes, I could, indeed, have healed Lazarus before He died.

But I am capable of so much more!

I AM the Resurrector! I can take what seems beyond hope and

breathe life back into it.

So bring to Me what feels lifeless. And if it is best for you, I will surely restore what you've lost.

But if I don't, keep in mind, My friend, that losses I allow are not meant to harm you but to bless you.

Can you believe that? Will you believe that? I love you enough let you suffer through having to let something... or someone go.

How can that be love?

Because just as was true for Lazarus and his sisters, the greater miracle may not be sparing you from suffering. The greater miracle may be breathing new life into what was lost. Sometimes that resurrection happens in Glory. But sometimes it happens in the here and now, especially when I'm testing your faith.

Whatever it is that feels like is slipping through your fingers, and you're getting anxious that I might just be too late – trust Me, My child... My friend. I'm doing what is truly for your ultimate good, and for My glory.

And I will do the greater miracle because I love you.

~ Digging Deeper ~

John 11:1-45, Isaiah 43:18-19, John 15:14-15, Romans 5:3-5

~ Questions to Consider ~

Where or how do you see God's love for you in today's Bible passages?

What else did you learn or were you reminded about God today?

Did you learn anything new about yourself or people in general from these passages?

~Personal Reflection ~

Are you currently asking the Lord to heal someone close to you, or rescue some circumstance in your life? What feels like it needs Jesus' healing touch today?

Do you truly trust God to do what's best for you, even if you don't really know what that might look like?

Is there something in your life that needs God's resurrection-power? A dream for the future? A relationship that seems damaged beyond repair? A heart crushed by circumstances you couldn't avoid or people you thought you could trust? What seems beyond hope, and needs the breath of life breathed back into it today?

~ Room to Respond ~

Is there something in you're asking God to save or heal right now that you need to surrender to His will?

_____

_____

_____

_____

_____

_____

_____

_____

_____

_____

_____

_____

_____

_____

~ Room to Respond ~

_____

_____

_____

_____

_____

_____

_____

_____

_____

_____

_____

_____

_____

_____

~ Day 21 ~

Safe Harbor for the Soul – from Psalm 27

"The LORD is my light and my salvation - whom shall I fear?
The LORD is the stronghold of my life - of whom shall I be afraid?"
Psalm 27:1 NIV

Are you feeling overwhelmed, child? Like you're caught on the sea in the midst of violent storm, with lightning endlessly flashing, thunder rattling your very bones, and churning waves crashing over your head… wave after wave till you cannot even catch your breath.

If that is you, My child, then I'm going to ask you to do something completely against your nature – look up! Away from the waves. Beyond the storm clouds. It's only natural to focus on what's frightening or overwhelming you. The storm is very real.

But remember this. Focus on this. **- I'm. Right. Here!**

Child, I am your Light and your Salvation. I am the Lighthouse offering you shelter and direction. You need never be anxious because I am the Fortress where you are protected in times of danger. So please don't be afraid.

Come closer to Me, instead. Close enough to hear My still, small voice above the deafening roar of the storm. The only way that can happen is when you seek one thing above all else…Me, your Savior and Friend. When you want nothing more than to dwell continually with Me, you'll find yourself delighting in My presence, meditating on My words, fixing your eyes only on Me.

Child, I am your Safe Harbor! And now that you've found refuge in Me, I want you to be a lighthouse too, standing on the shore, shining your light, My light, for all to see. Then they, too, will be able to find their way through the fog and storms of life. Guide them here to Me. Use your light to show them the way. And sound your voice to alert them to the dangers along the journey.

I have placed you here in My harbor on the Solid Rock. So stand firm and steady… and shine!

~ Digging Deeper ~

Psalm 27, 1 Kings 19:11-13, Psalm 46:1-5, Isaiah 32:2, Jeremiah 29:12-14, Matthew 5:14-16

Note: the Hebrew word for stronghold in Psalm 27:1 is "maoz," meaning "a place or means of safety, protection, refuge, stronghold — a harbor (biblehub.com)

~ Questions to Consider ~

Where or how do you see God's love for you in today's Bible passages?

What else did you learn or were you reminded about God today?

Did you learn anything new about yourself or people in general from these passages?

~ **Personal Reflection** ~

Do you feel like you're caught in a storm right now? How does that feel?

Have you ever seen a lighthouse, or perhaps a picture of one? What are its distinctive features? What purpose does it serve?

What parallels can you draw between a lighthouse and Jesus? And do you believe you can be a lighthouse, too?

Read Isaiah 32:2 with a lighthouse in mind. While this passage is referring to a future time, are these things we could strive for now? Can you think of someone you know who needs a spiritual lighthouse? Are you willing to fill that roll?

~ Room to Respond ~

~ *Day 22* ~

On Your Side – from Psalm 124

"If the LORD had not been on our side –
…if the LORD had not been on our side…
then they would have swallowed us alive…"
Psalm 124:1-3 CSB

I am on your side, My child.

Let Me say that one more time so it really sinks in - I. Am. On. Your. Side!

Is it hard for you to see that right now? Is it hard to believe, when your enemy is closing in, has you surrounded, and is threatening to swallow you alive… is it hard to believe that I'm here for you? That I'm closer to you than even your next breath? That I will rescue you at just the right time?

Oh child…I know you're feeling so overwhelmed. And that's why I want to remind you that I'm right here. I take sides. And the one I'm on is yours.

I have seen all you're going through. I feel your tension and anxiety, like a little bird caught in a net you couldn't see coming. You've fought so hard to get free, but in doing so only found yourself more entangled than ever.

And that's precisely why I'm here.

I am the one who can free you. In fact, I have already cut the net so you can escape. When My Son Jesus rose from His grave, He broke every chain that binds you, every net that ensnares you. He made a way for your freedom.

But you'll only find your way to that freedom, My child, if you listen for His gentle voice leading you to the opening He has made for you. It's plenty big. And I'll be there to keep the net from catching your wings as you fly free.

And when you do, when you finally break free of all that's entangled you, remember I am your helper and friend. I am the one who made all you see. And that means I have the power to say to those crashing waves, "Peace. Be still." And to the enemy that had you surrounded, "You have no power here."

You are My child. And as long as you draw breath, I will always be on your side, ready to help you. Ready to free you. Ready to pull you in close enough to hide in Me.

Yes, I have chosen a side, and it's yours.

But what about you? Have you chosen a side yet? The best one, the only truly perfect one is Mine. And there's plenty of room for you here.

~ Digging Deeper ~

Psalm 124, Psalm 46:1-5, Psalm 56:9-11, Psalm 118:6-7, Romans 8:31

~ Questions to Consider ~

Where or how do you see God's love for you in today's Bible passages?

What else did you learn or were you reminded about God today?

Did you learn anything new about yourself or people in general from these passages?

~ **Personal Reflection** ~

Have you ever felt like you were completely surrounded, with no one on your side? What were the circumstances?

Do you believe the Lord was on your side, even though it might not have felt like it? How might that confidence help you through difficult situations?

How can you know for sure that God really is on your side? What assurance do you have?

Is it possible you're not yet on God's side? If not, please see the note in the appendix about beginning that relationship with Him.

~ Room to Respond ~

~ Room to Respond ~

_____

_____

_____

_____

_____

_____

_____

_____

_____

_____

_____

_____

_____

_____

~ *Day 23* ~

Follow Me Marks – from John 20

*"...[Jesus] saw Simon and Andrew, Simon's brother, casting a net into the sea –
for they were fishermen. 'Follow me,' Jesus told them, 'and I will make you fish for
people.' And immediately they left their nets and followed him."*
Mark 1:16-18 CSB

Did you know I created many animal species with something called
"follow me" marks? These distinctive colors and patterns make them
easily identifiable to their young. So when the enemy comes prowling,
they recognize exactly whom they should follow to safety.

But they're not the only ones with "follow me" marks. My son Jesus
has them, too!

That has not always been the case. They were cruelly nailed into His
hands and feet, and pierced deeply into His side when He died on the
cross for your sins. It was those scars from His death that helped His
disciples better identify Him after He rose from the dead.

And those scars are what give Him and Me the right to offer you life
with Us for eternity.

But even before He died, Jesus was marked by other things -
goodness, grace, mercy, forgiveness and love, even for His enemies. No
one before Him was ever marked in such a remarkable way.

So even though you cannot physically see Jesus' nail-pierced hands
and feet, you can see in My Word exactly who He was. And if you
listen, you will still hear that same call He gave His first century
disciples – "Follow Me!"

And when His Spirit is alive in you, when you've accepted His
follow-Me call, you can then display those very same traits He
demonstrated so perfectly. Then others will be able to follow you to
find Me because you're wearing His unmistakable marks, especially
love.

But please beware. There are many false teachers out there without the marks of Jesus. They'll try to convince you that what they're saying comes from Me. Their messages sound pretty good. They tell people exactly what they want to hear, and that makes them feel good about themselves. But if you listen carefully, and compare what they say with My Word, you will see for yourself their message is not Mine at all. It is worldly and deceptive, leading those who are deceived in a completely wrong direction. If you're confused by someone's message, feeling a nudge that something's not quite right, find the "follow Me" marks in My Word. It will always speak truth and lead you in the right direction, closer to Me.

You should also be aware that your enemy, the devil, can also see My mark on you. So you may hear him prowling nearby. If that happens, there's no need to panic. My Spirit in you will always be greater and stronger than any spirit in this world. And I will not let the enemy go beyond what I strengthen and empower you to bear.

So, child, remember when you're facing unfamiliar territory, an unrelenting enemy, or teaching that just doesn't add up, look for the "follow Me" marks in My Word and in My Son. They're not hard to recognize. And will always lead you to the Truth. To Me.

~ Digging Deeper ~

John 20:19-39, Mark 1:16-20, Luke 5:37-38, Acts 17:11-13, 1 Corinthians 10:13, 2 Corinthians 11:12-15, 2 Timothy 4:3-4, Hebrews 4:12, 1 Peter 5:8, 1 John 4:1-4

~ Questions to Consider ~

Where or how do you see God's love for you in today's Bible passages?

What else did you learn or were you reminded about God today?

Did you learn anything new about yourself or people in general from these passages?

~ Personal Reflection ~

Were you already aware that there are many false teachers? Have you already encountered some? What do they look and sound like? (see 2 Corinthians 11:12-15)

Where might you find them?

If you're feeling that nudge that some teaching you've heard or read outside the Bible isn't quite right, what should you do about it? How can you find the truth?

While we cannot not see Jesus yet, we are able to see His marks in others. What traits can we look for to know if someone has the Spirit of God in them?

What does it look like to follow Jesus, not just as a one-time decision of surrender, but also as a daily decision to let Him lead?

~ Room to Respond ~

~ Room to Respond ~

_____

_____

_____

_____

_____

_____

_____

_____

_____

_____

_____

_____

_____

_____

~ *Day 24* ~

Here for You – from Psalm 68

*"God in his holy dwelling is a father of the fatherless
and a champion of widows. God provides homes
for those who are deserted..." Psalm 68:5-6 CSB*

My child, if ever you're feeling unseen, unloved, or all alone, remember I'm right here with you. I know you can't really see Me or hear Me. But if you look closely, you can see what I'm doing all around you. You can see evidence that I'm here in doors that open for you, or sometimes those that close. When there's suddenly a way when there was no way before, leading you closer to My side… that's Me.

It's kind of like the wind. You can't see it. But you can see where it's moving in the tossing flowers or swaying trees. White caps on the water let you know the wind is getting stronger as it passes through. And I'm just as real. Just as present. Just as active in your life.

I'm here for you!

Maybe friends and family have walked away. Or perhaps they've been taken from you. Maybe you've lost something precious. Someone precious. And you are that deserted one in desperate need of a job, a home, a family, a friend.

It may be hard to grasp this truth, but it is truth nonetheless – I can be all of those for you. When all else fails, child, I desire to be all you need. And I can be only if you'll let Me. If you'll seek for Me with all your heart, I promise I'll make Myself more real to you than you've ever experienced.

And when you finally find Me, as you see Me moving and acting on your behalf, I will have the ultimate pleasure of hearing you sing praises back to Me. You will at last discover the deep and abiding joy of My presence. So sing out strong, and share with the world what it's like to know Me. Really know Me. So few do. So few care to.

Perhaps if they could finally see Me because they see Me in you…wouldn't that be something?! You could be that tree swaying with the wind of my Spirit. Did you know wind and spirit are from the same original word? How fitting, don't you think.

So child, close your eyes and feel the Spirit move in you. Let Us be all you need and more. We are here for you!

~ Digging Deeper ~

Psalm 68:3-6 & 32-35, Psalm 10:14, 16-18, Psalm 62, Jeremiah 29:12-14, John 3:8, Hebrews 13:5

~ Questions to Consider ~

Where or how do you see God's love for you in today's Bible passages?

What else did you learn or were you reminded about God today?

Did you learn anything new about yourself or people in general from these passages?

~ **Personal Reflections** ~

Do you know God's Spirit is real in your life? How do you know? What evidence have you seen of His presence?

Have there been times when you struggled to sense God's presence? What can you do when you feel that way?

Are there verses that help you refocus on the reality of His moving in your life?

~ Room to Respond ~

~ Room to Respond ~

~ *Day 25* ~

No Place Too Far – from Psalm 139

"I'm never out of your sight…
I look behind me and you're there, then up ahead and you're there, too -
your reassuring presence, coming and going.
This is too much, too wonderful — I can't take it all in!"
Psalm 139:3-6 MSG

Did you know, child, there is no place you can go that I'm not already there? I hope that encourages your heart today.

I realize My constant presence can at times feel like a blessing; but other times, not so much.

Just ask My prophet, Jonah. When he was frustrated and angry about what I asked him to do, he tried to run from Me. He hopped in a boat and literally headed in the opposite direction.

And what about Adam and Eve in the Garden of Eden? When they disobeyed and did the very thing I instructed them not to do, they tried to hide from Me, too.

But because I love so deeply, I went looking for them. I knew right where to find them since I was already there with them. They just couldn't see Me through all their fear and shame.

And because I had a purpose in My plan for Jonah, I went looking for him too. I even created a special creature of the deep to protect and carry him to safety, although that's not likely how it felt at the time. The slimy insides of a giant fish probably felt more like a punishing prison than protection.

And maybe you're feeling those things today too – the shame, and fear, and isolation that come with distance from Me.

But child, I want you to hear this loud and clear today – I am already here, right beside you. All around you. Even within you because that's who I am, and always will be. Immanuel…God with you.

I already know what you did. Where you've gone. And just how you feel.

So I'm not here to condemn you. I'm here to restore you!

My presence should not cause you to run further in your shame or bury yourself deeper in your pain. Look at Me, child. Look up, and see the love, forgiveness, mercy, grace, and acceptance in My eyes. You are My precious child, and I long to hold you close; not see you struggle in your pain.

Just as I covered Jonah in the belly of the fish, and Adam and Eve with animal skins, I am here to cover you, too. My unfailing love can do that. It already has.

The shadow of My Son's sacrifice on the cross covers you even now. His shed blood blankets and smothers the condemnation. And His victory over death frees you to throw off your shame. So don't hide in that shadow; find your peace there.

Find it in Me, because I AM your peace. And your joy in knowing there's no place too far that My grace can't reach.

~ Digging Deeper ~

Psalm 139:1-12, Genesis 3:6-9 & 21, Isaiah 59:1-2 & 20-21, Jonah 1:1-3, 1:17-2:10, Isaiah 7:14/ Matthew 1:23, Romans 8:1, Ephesians 2:14

~ Questions to Consider ~

Have you ever wanted to hide from God? What were the circumstances?

Did He come looking for you?

Do you trust that what God wants for you is ultimately what's best for you? If not, what makes it difficult to believe?

If you're enjoying a healthy relationship with God, but have friends or family who have drifted from Him, how might you be able to encourage them to get things back on track? Remember, it's not too far for them, either.

~ Room to Respond ~

~ *Day 26* ~

Why Do You Ask? – from Jeremiah 42

*"Pray that the LORD your God will show us what to do and where to go.
Whether we like it or not, we will obey the LORD our God…"
"And today I [Jeremiah] have told you exactly what he said,
but you will not obey…" Jeremiah 42:3,6,21 CSB*

I love when you come to Me for guidance, My child. That's just the way it's meant to be between fathers and their children. Fathers have deep wisdom that comes from many years of experience. And as your *Heavenly* Father, My wisdom is magnified far beyond any human understanding. So it pleases Me immensely to have you come to Me.

But please keep this in mind, My seeking one – there have been many in the past who've come for guidance only to reject My advice and do things their own way. They simply wanted to know My will without having any intention of doing it.

And that breaks My heart. Not just because disobeying one's father is challenging his word. But because it reveals a deep lack of trust. If they truly trusted that I had their best interest at heart, they would follow My lead.

You, My child, are in that very valley of decision.

Will you ask for My advice? And is it your heart's deepest desire to then follow?

It's good to check your heart carefully. Those who've strayed had not intended to do so from the start. But when My will didn't match what they had already set their minds to, they turned from Me. They even tried to convince themselves that perhaps they hadn't heard right.

Are you willing, My child, to truly listen for My voice…no matter what message it brings?

It may challenge your sense of comfort. It may even seem unreasonable, but only in human terms. So don't turn away when My leading doesn't seem to make sense. If it always did, I would be a god no bigger than your brain.

But I'm so much bigger, and can see so much further. So trust Me, child. Seek My will, then take the next step in that direction.

I will be holding your hand the entire way!

~ Digging Deeper ~

Jeremiah 42, Isaiah 55:6-9, Matthew 7:24-27, James 1:5-8

~ Questions to Consider ~

Where or how do you see God's love for you in today's Bible passages?

What else did you learn or were you reminded about God today?

Did you learn anything new about yourself or people in general from these passages?

~ **Personal Reflection** ~

Is there some area in your life where you could use divine direction?

Do you ever find yourself already down the road of your own choosing before remembering to ask God what He might want? Are you there now?

Is God the first one you go to when you need advice? If not, why not?

Why does it often seem easier to ask the people around you first?

Have you ever sensed God wanting you to go one direction, but you chose another? How did that turn out? What led you to make that choice? Would you do the same thing again under the same circumstances?

~ **Room to Respond** ~

~ Room to Respond ~

~ *Day 27* ~

Look Up – from Psalm 3

*"But you, LORD, are a shield around me,
my glory, and the one who lifts up my head."*
Psalm 3:3 CSB

Did you know there's a story about My children being surrounded by poisonous snakes in the wilderness? As they were suffering, I heard their desperate cries and rescued them. But the rescue required a huge challenge. The only way to be saved from the snakes was by looking up at a bronze snake on a pole. This challenged their faith, as they had to choose to either focus on their fears or trust Me instead.

Right now, child, you may feel like you're surrounded by circumstances beyond your control, with no way out. And the enemy of your soul is fueling the fire, hissing in your ear that I either don't care about you or am powerless to help you. You hear the rattles of your worst fears and it draws your complete attention to your daunting situation. You feel you haven't the courage or strength to do anything but dodge venomous snakes.

But I'm right here with you, child. If you would just look up from your fears and focus on Me - the author and perfecter of your faith. Feel My hand beneath your chin, helping you lift that worry-weary head above the mess surrounding you.

I have heard you cry out to Me. And I will be a shield surrounding you with My all-powerful presence. My love, compassion, strength and wisdom are all you need to survive. To thrive! The power to rescue is in My mighty right hand. And the will to rescue is in My gracious heart.

So look up. Look to Me! I am rising up to save you, even now.

Salvation is Mine to give. Rest and peace of mind will follow. You'll see. Let fear fall away as your gaze meets Mine, full of love for you. Then stay focused here on Me.

And when you feel you cannot even so much as lift your eyes, let alone your head…simply whisper My name. And I will lift it for you.

~ Digging Deeper ~

Psalm 3, Numbers 21:4-9, Psalm 27:4-6, John 3:14-15, Hebrews 12:2

~ Questions to Consider ~

Where or how do you see God's love for you in today's Bible passages?

What else did you learn or were you reminded about God today?

Did you learn anything new about yourself or people in general from these passages?

~Personal Reflection ~

Have you ever been so paralyzed by fear, anxiety, or weariness that you didn't know what to do? What were the circumstances? Is that where you are today?

What circumstances demand your attention and keep you from looking up to Jesus?

There is a link between Numbers 21:4-9 and John 3:14-15. What is it?

If you were to look straight up into the eyes of Jesus right now, what do you think you'd see?

Did you give it a try? If you did, share what you saw there, how you felt.

~ Room to Respond ~

_____

_____

_____

_____

_____

_____

_____

_____

_____

_____

_____

_____

_____

~ *Day 28* ~

Even When – from Psalm 23

*"Even when I walk through the darkest valley,
I will not be afraid, for you are close beside me."*
Psalm 23:4a NLT

My child, I've asked you to let Me lead. I've asked you to trust that I'm a good Shepherd. *Your* good Shepherd. And yet, here we are in the darkest valley you've ever known. I know it's hard to understand how a good God could let this happen.

So I need you to slide in close. Close enough to feel the steady rhythm of My heart. And hear Me say, "I love you!"

Even this valley is Me saying, "I love you."

I'm sure you're wondering how that could possibly be true. But I assure you it is. I will use even the lowest valleys and darkest nights to stretch your faith, and help you learn to trust Me even more. That may seem unlikely in the moment. But you'll see. And you'll marvel at My goodness and faithfulness, even in this.

And once you've made it through the valley, you'll find a feast of blessings waiting for you on the other side. It's already prepared with all the trimmings, all you need for healing and restoration. Your enemies will watch and wonder at the joy you've found, even in the midst of such a difficult journey. They may even get splashed a bit by the overflow. I hope you'll remember this promise and smile when you see it fulfilled.

In the meantime, child, I feel I should warn you that something is chasing you. But please slow down. Because what's pursuing you is My goodness and faithful love. Let it catch you and overwhelm you! It's just a foretaste of all you'll enjoy one day in Heaven with Me.

What a day that will be! I can't wait!

~ Digging Deeper ~

Psalm 23, Job 37:1-13, Jeremiah 29:11, John 11:1-45 (especially 5-6)

~ Questions to Consider ~

Where or how do you see God's love for you in today's Bible passages?

What else did you learn or were you reminded about God today?

Did you learn anything new about yourself or people in general from these passages?

~ **Personal Reflection** ~

If you're in a valley right now, describe what it looks like, how it feels.

Have valleys in your life caused you to doubt the goodness of God?

Where might that doubt be coming from?

What is currently weighing on you? Overwhelming you? Pursuing you?

Have you ever imagined what it feels like to be pursued by goodness? Especially the goodness of God? Describe what it might feel like to slow down and allow God's goodness and mercy to catch up with you.

~ Room to Respond ~

_____

_____

_____

_____

_____

_____

_____

_____

_____

_____

_____

_____

_____

~ *Day 29* ~

This Is the Way – from Psalm 16

*"I always let the Lord guide me.
Because he is at my right hand, I will not be shaken.
You reveal the path of life to me; in your presence is abundant joy;
at your right hand are eternal pleasures.
Psalm 16:8,11 CSB*

Where are you headed, My child? What are your plans for this year?
This week? Today?

Did you know I have a plan for you?

The world is more than happy to suggest ideas for your future, to
share their views of success, happiness, normalcy. They are ready and
willing to point the way. But child, My desires for you are so much
different. And I would love to show you the way.

Now child, you may be asking, "How can we know the way?" And
you won't be the first to ask. My answer is still the same as it was many
centuries ago - I AM the way!

I know that's probably not the answer you were hoping for. You
want to know what's next, what My specific plans are for you; at least
you think you do. But rather than investing all your time trying to
uncover My plan, try uncovering My heart instead. Get to know Me.
Live daily in obedience to what you already know I would ask of you.
Love Me and love others. Be kind and forgiving. Remain faithful. Do
what My Word teaches you is right. Make time for Me!

Here's the thing, child - obedience is one of My love languages. And
when you're following what I've already revealed, you'll also find a
peace and joy that the world, with all its promises of success, can never
give you.

Pursuing worldly direction and happiness will lead to comparison,
frustration, anxiety, and ultimately an emptiness in that hole that only I
was meant to fill.

It's when you pursue a relationship with Me through time in My

Word, or sharing your heart with Me in prayer and listening to Mine, even in spending time with My other children... it's there you'll find you're on the right path. Doors that match the gifts I've given you will open. Doors that aren't a good fit for you will close. Please let them; and recognize that's My leading as well. It's not rejection. It's redirection.

Ultimately My plan for you is abundant joy both in the next life, and this one too. You don't have to wait for Heaven to be happy. You can be happy in Me now. Won't you?

My greatest desire is that *I* would be your plan, your pursuit, your passion. And when that happens, My child, you'll find the doors to your heart's desires will begin to open like never before. And that's because your plans will finally match Mine.

You'll find your way when you finally find Me. I can't wait!

~ Digging Deeper ~

Psalm 16, Psalm 37:3-7, Isaiah 30:21, Jeremiah 29:11-14, Matthew 6:33, John 10:10, John 14:5-6,14-15&27, John 15:1-17

~ Questions to Consider ~

Where or how do you see God's love for you in today's Bible passages?

What else did you learn or were you reminded about God today?

Did you learn anything new about yourself or people in general from these passages?

~ **Personal Reflection** ~

What makes you happy? Are you satisfied with the direction in which you're heading?

Does God fit in with that pursuit? How?

Have you been asking God for direction? How might you pursue that differently now?

~ Room to Respond ~

~ Room to Respond ~

_____

_____

_____

_____

_____

_____

_____

_____

_____

_____

_____

_____

_____

_____

~ Day 30 ~

You Smell So Good! – from 2 Corinthians 2

*"For we are to God the pleasing aroma of Christ among those
who are being saved and those who are perishing."*
2 Corinthians 2:15 NIV

Do you know someone who has kept a piece of clothing, maybe a blanket, or scarf, or shirt that belonged to someone they loved just because it smelled like them? What do you suppose happens when they breathe in that familiar fragrance? I've seen it – that knowing, remembering smile as if they're suddenly transported right into the presence of the one whose scent it bears.

Scents can do that. And it's part of the reason I designed you the way I did. I want you to connect deeply with those I've brought into your life. So deeply that even a familiar fragrance passing by reminds you of them and how much love you've shared.

Have you ever stopped to consider that I might do the same with My Son, My One and Only? When I see you acting like Him – loving those around you, including your enemies, and when I hear you talking like Him – encouraging others, helping them find peace and joy, when you say and do things that remind Me of Him, it's as if I've taken a deep breath, and find His familiar scent lingering on you.

And it brings Me such joy!

Have you read in the Old Testament of the sacrifices people would bring to My temple? So much of the sacrificial system reminded Me of My Son, and His sacrifice that would come. And while there would be much suffering and sorrow, We both knew the joy that His death and resurrection would bring. So the incense waived before Me along with the smoke that rose to My throne room…all were pleasing aromas because of what they pointed to. Who they pointed to.

Child, the sacrifices you make even today in Jesus' name still do the same. And when you tell others about Me and My Son, that helps spread the aroma even further.

Now, I must warn you – not everyone will find it a pleasing fragrance. Those who have turned their backs on Me may actually find it offensive, sensing death in the lingering scent. That's because they don't have life in Me.

At least not yet.

But those who do know and love Me…they will lift their faces to breathe deeply of the aroma of Jesus pouring out from you. To them, it is the fragrance of life!

So let it pour! Let others see, and hear, and even smell the Me in you. Let your words and deeds spread the essence of Jesus to the world around you.   And as the sweetness in the air reaches My throne, I will look at My Son with the greatest pride and joy a father can have. Then I will point to you and say to Him, "Look, Son…this one reminds Me so much of You."

~ Digging Deeper ~

2 Corinthians 2:14-17, Leviticus 1:9,13&17, Psalm 51:16-17, Isaiah 58:3-7, Malachi 1:8-13

~ Questions to Consider ~

Where or how do you see God's love for you in today's Bible passages?

What else did you learn or were you reminded about God today?

Did you learn anything new about yourself or people in general from these passages?

~ **Personal Reflection** ~

Have you kept something because it reminds you of someone you love? How does it remind you of them?

What might others think of Jesus based on the way you act or speak to them?

What have you said or done recently that might have been a pleasing aroma to your Heavenly Father?

Do you think there are things we say and do that might be an offensive odor to Him? (see Psalm 51:16-17, Isaiah 58:3-7, Malachi 1:8-13)

What can you do today that would remind God of His Son Jesus?

~ **Room to Respond** ~

~ Room to Respond ~

_____

_____

_____

_____

_____

_____

_____

_____

_____

_____

_____

_____

_____

Giving Your Life to Jesus

The scriptures and poems in this book are full of encouragement and promises for those who call Jesus Christ their Lord and Savior. If you have never made that commitment and would like to, here's what you can do to start a personal relationship with God:

God loves you! and wants you to have a real, personal relationship with Him where you can talk to Him and hear from Him every day; and after this life, spend eternity in Heaven with Him.

"For this is how God loved the world: He gave his one and only Son, so that everyone who believes in him will not perish but have eternal life." John 3:16 NLT

But you and I are sinners – that means we fall short of God's mark of perfection. We do things that are wrong, we ignore God, and we try to find our fulfillment, joy, and peace everywhere but in God. So **our sin and pride separate us from God**, and from experiencing His love and plan for our lives.

"For everyone has sinned; we all fall short of God's glorious standard." Romans 3:23 NLT

"For the wages of sin is death, but the free gift of God is eternal life through Christ Jesus our Lord." Romans 6:23 NLT

The best news ever is that **Jesus made a way**! Our sin earned us a death sentence, eternal separation from God. But He came down from Heaven and died a cruel death on a cross to pay that penalty for us. The best part is He didn't stay dead… He came back to life showing us that He has power over both sin and death – the power to offer us forgiveness, grace (His underserved favor), and eternal life as a gift.

"But God showed his great love for us by sending Christ to die for us while we were still sinners." Romans 5:8 NLT

"Christ suffered for our sins once for all time. He never sinned, but he died for sinners to bring you safely home to God. He suffered physical death, but he was raised to life in the Spirit." 1 Peter 3:18 NLT

All that's left for us to do in order to have eternal life in Heaven, and a relationship with God now, while still on earth, is to **receive that amazing gift** He offers. We do that by acknowledging that we are indeed sinners, in need of a Savior; and that Jesus did what we could not – in His sinlessness, He paid our penalty in full when He died on the cross. God says

"If you openly declare that Jesus is Lord and believe in your heart that God raised him from the dead, you will be saved." Romans 10:9 NLT

Declaring Jesus as Lord means we turn away from our sins, and surrender our hearts and lives to Him. God's desire is that we would love Him "*with all your heart, all your soul, and all your mind.*" (Matthew 22:37 NLT)

The offer has been extended to you, and the choice is yours. Are you ready to receive God's gift of salvation through His Son Jesus? It's the best decision you'll ever make! He has great plans for you...

"God saved you by his grace when you believed. And you can't take credit for this; it is a gift from God. Salvation is not a reward for the good things we have done, so none of us can boast about it. For we are God's masterpiece. He has created us anew in Christ Jesus, so we can do the good things he planned for us long ago." Ephesians 2:8-10 NLT

My prayer is that if you do not yet know Jesus as your Savior, that you will accept His gift of salvation this very day! If you do, there will be great rejoicing in Heaven, and I will see you there one day.

INDEX of DEVOTIONS

Love, God

INDEX of SCRIPTURES

Psalms

ABOUT THE AUTHOR

Lisa (Kesinger) DeVinney was born in rural Indiana in 1966; and raised in a Christian home. At the age of seven, she gave her heart to Jesus Christ.

When Lisa was twelve years old, her father answered God's call to full time ministry; so she and her siblings spent their teenage years as a pastor's kids in Skaneateles, New York.

Following high school, Lisa spent two years at Houghton College, majoring in Math and Education. And during that time, Lisa married her best friend, Dan, whom she'd known since sixth grade. At the end of that year, his job took them to western New York.

Over the next nine years, God blessed Dan and Lisa with six children: five boys, followed by a baby girl. Lisa stayed home with the kids as they moved from New York to North Carolina, and back again to New York. All the kids played sports through high school, and some in college. So Lisa spent lots of time as a sports mom, and loved every minute of it!

After their youngest child graduated from high school, God surprised Dan and Lisa with a call to full-time college ministry with the Fellowship of Christian Athletes. They are serving in southern Pennsylvania where Lisa has the opportunity to use her passions for teaching, baking, and photography to minister to students and coaches at Millersville University.

It is Lisa's desire and prayer that God would use these devotions to draw hearts closer to Him. There is, after all, no greater pursuit in this life than that of a closer relationship with the one true God!

If you'd like to connect with Lisa, you will find her active on Facebook and Instagram, or at her website lisadevinney.org.

OTHER TITLES by Lisa DeVinney

Sunday School Lessons 2012 -
Followers of God, 3ʳᵈ-6ᵗʰ Grade Level

Great Men and Women of the Bible

I Will Lift Up Mine Eyes:
366 Daily Devotionals in Poetry and Scripture

Rivers in the Desert:
366 Daily Devotionals in Poetry and Scripture

Blessings in the Rain:
90 Days of Encouragement Through the Storm

ACKNOWLEDGEMENTS

"Every time I think of you, I give thanks to my God...
for you have been my partners in spreading the Good News
about Christ from the time you first heard it until now.
And I am certain that God, who began the good work...will continue his work
until it is finally finished on the day when Christ Jesus returns.
So it is right that I should feel as I do about all of you,
for you have a special place in my heart."
Philippians 1:3-7a NLT

From the very beginning, this devotional has been bathed in prayer, and not just by me. I had a whole team of pray-ers behind and beside me throughout the process keeping me motivated, encouraged, and focused on the mission – making this Bible reading tool available to those whose faith journeys could use a little spark.

So THANK YOU Amy Decker, Amy (Kesinger) Pope, Barbie Teboe, Cathy (Kesinger) Sankey, Cindy Tamboso, Dana Morehouse, Debbie Dufek, Sharon Niese, and Tracy Newman. I love you all and cannot thank you enough for being my prayer-warriors and website cheerleaders!

I also needed a scholarly eye to help me keep the content in line with Scripture. And who better to do that than my own favorite pastor and his wife who also happen to be the world's best parents, Rev. Tom & Jan Kesinger. Thanks for keeping me in line once again, Mom and Dad. I have learned so much from both of you! And I hope it shows.

When it came to designing the cover, I desperately needed a younger, hipper eye. My daughter Danni stepped in to take my grandmotherly design and transform it into a cover a twenty-something young lady would consider picking up for herself. Thanks, Danni! Your patience with me through the process has been incredible and so appreciated.

And lastly, books don't get finished without the time and encouragement to do so. This final thank you is to my best friend, biggest cheerleader, and husband, Dan, who has given me the freedom to devote needed time to this project. I love you, Bud! And am so thankful God knew just who I needed to walk alongside me in this journey.

Love, God

Made in the USA
Middletown, DE
25 September 2025

17444557R10113